REAWAKENING
a BOOK OF LIFE & A STORY BEYOND TIME

Howard Lawrence Scheiner, MD/AAHIVS

authorHOUSE®

AuthorHouse™
1663 Liberty Drive
Bloomington, IN 47403
www.authorhouse.com
Phone: 1-800-839-8640

First published by AuthorHouse   4/22/2011

ISBN: 978-1-4567-5487-7 (sc)
ISBN: 978-1-4567-5486-0 (hc)
ISBN: 978-1-4567-5485-3 (e)

Library of Congress Control Number: 2011904248

Printed in the United States of America

for Domingo,

a Book of LIFE

Welcome to a Greater Reality

Love & Light,

Howard

Howard Lawrence Scheiner, MD/AAHIVS

CONTENTS

A BOOK OF LIFE

FORGETTING AND REMEMBERANCE

DEDICATION

I want to dedicate this book first and foremost to my parents. They are the most wonderful parents I could have ever chosen; they have loved, supported, and allowed my life to be all that it could be. Likewise, my good and loving brother Steven.

I am especially grateful to all my grandparents (William, Eva, Max, and Sophie) who endured and sacrificed so much to bring their families to America's shore.

For well over half my life, there has been a constant—my medical partner in our practice and my friend for almost forty years—Kenneth Schaefer, MD. Since there is probably no one else who has shared and endured so much of my life's travails, I wanted to acknowledge his unwavering support, kind heart, and great love. He remains my rock of stability in a life of turmoil, without whom I would have a very different life than this one I am following.

And given the chance, I would not change a thing!

PREFACE

I wrote this to share my experience, mainly with my family and friends. If I can add to the love and light in the world, letting my story resonate with all who might find it consistent with their own understandings or experiences, that is an additional bonus. In writing this book, I am also following my childlike/godlike dream without boundary—to be a beacon of light—to connect people across the planet, so diverse in so many countless personalities, to share in a resonant commonality of the truth of a greater reality.

In writing this book, the themes found in the preceding sketch, given to me over thirty-five years ago by my parents, seem almost prophetic to me. What is truly predestined? What makes for a happy life or a successful life? These, my dears, are the threads that are woven into the fabric of my story...

Anyone who has seen the film "The Matrix" understands "Matrix Philosophy". Do you choose the red pill, which will answer "The Question", or do you choose the blue pill which allows life to simply carry on as before? To paraphrase the words of Morpheus from the film, "All I'm offering is the truth. Nothing more."

And what is the truth? It encompasses the meaning and the purpose of life and embraces an understanding of a greater reality. One would think that everyone would want to know truth. But it is not quite so simple. We can't all quite handle truth. But that's life!

All roads lead to the same destination. The train each travels is set on its course. While I have neither the desire nor the ability to change anyone's journey, I do believe I can offer a travel upgrade. It is possible to travel in greater comfort in a more luxurious carriage, with larger windows that give a greater view of the beautiful vistas along the way.

I have no desire, nor am I attempting to convert, proselytize, or convince anyone of anything that does not feel true to them. So, I share my story of love and discovery and hope that it finds resonance in your hearts.

Although I use the word God many times from the earliest pages of this book, I purposefully try to avoid dwelling on the word, or on the understanding of that word "God". God has gotten such awful press in large part thanks or no thanks to religion. It is usually not a word mentioned in polite conversation unless you are a "true" religious figure, a religious zealot, fanatic, evangelical, or just some really weird person from the fringes of society. The exception, of course, is if you are cursing God, or when "God Damn It" seems an appropriate epithet to use. Then, it is perfectly fine. So, whether you are an atheist, agnostic, or subscribe to any religion or not, don't worry about God for now, either as a concept or a word. I ask your willing suspension of belief or disbelief. If you have any resistance to this word, it would be helpful if you can set it aside for the moment. For now, make any human image you may wish, or imagine any force that you would hope God to be.

PROLOGUE

Gabriel—So, I was out with a friend drinking beer. Got home tipsy-to-drunk… went and got a slice of pizza and ate it on my stoop. And realized how far I've fallen. I'm pathetic. I was a proud 20-something year old. I proved my skills, my intelligence, empathy, trust, and more without any degree. But that's not the case anymore.

My plan not only blew up in my face but sent a ripple, well no actually a 9.8 shockwave through my circle of friends…my great planning once again failed me like it did when I was once accepted to medical school. Every day I think, what's the point of making an effort to reach any goal when life continues to fuck me and those I love?

I feel unworthy and pathetic when it comes to pursuing any sort of romantic interest. I would never date me, not ever in this state. This puts me in a place of complete loneliness and rightfully so. And no, I'm not depressed or suicidal or anything like that. I'm just tired.

I think of this every waking moment. Hell, I dream about it constantly. I wake in the middle of the night to take a sleeping pill or Xanax to try to calm my mind and rest easy… though it's rare that I do.

I'm not sure why I'm telling you this. I don't even know how I'll respond to any feedback. I get testy when we talk about it because talking about it when we're out and about is overwhelming after trying to figure out an alternative all fucking day.

I guess I just need you to understand why sometimes I'd rather sleep, don't want to talk, or do want to talk… why I obsess over new cute guys…and why other days I need to be alone.

Well I can try to sum it up. Here goes:
    Pain
    Regret
    Mooch
    Pathetic

Stupid
Unintelligent
Overwhelmed
Hurt
Lost
Disgusted w/self
Very lonely
Unworthy
& Again Pain
There's more but that's the gist.

Michael—I can't tell you how much I feel like I want to say "fuck all" and push aside my other social plans tomorrow, run up to Spanish Harlem to see him, buy some poppers/weed/get drunk and have unprotected wild sex and fuck and be fucked like rabbits and orgasm four times. Seriously. I've done it before and I feel this intimacy, this power, this validation that I'm attractive and I feel like I'm in control. I just want to be a hot guy like the guys on the cover of NEXT magazine, like the guys at my gym, like the guys at the bars I've worked at. A part of me just wants to be hot and stupid and live a pointless life working in bars and doing photo shoots.

But then my other passions (art) kick in and the knowledge that unsafe health practices are not good. But I feel like this moth that keeps wanting to get close to the flame and I keep wanting to get close and I should just let myself go there. I've never been to a rave and been on coke or ecstasy. I've always been really responsible. I've always said "my career is too important." My career has given me so much of the growth I've wanted as a person, but it still hasn't made me happy or taken off. So it's like, "if I'm unhappy anyway, why not just have some fun?"

I can step back and say it's not my career that's too important, it's that I'm too important. But too important for what? To have fun?

As a teenager I thought "I'm going to be better than my peers and not drink or do drugs." I'm going to be a "career" person and settle down (and I did). And then at 22, I was like, "fuck the settling down, I'm exploring." But I've still held on to "I'm not going to party, that's just stupid." I really want to do it.

But then my work does give me rushes with plans of steady happiness (even though it's bringing me minimal income) and I don't want all my practice and discipline to go out the window because I'm on drugs and addicted to some really bad stuff. And kicking a coke addiction is not something I ever want on my to-do list. I have been encouraged to put together a business plan for a show idea I have and I've shared parts of it with a couple of his friends already and they want to introduce me to people who might invest. This could be just another plan that's gonna go nowhere. Or this could be "it" for me.

I don't want a sense of superiority to be the reason I don't party and I don't want safety-town to be the reason I don't have unprotected sex. I want love to be the reason I don't and don't even think about it. But is loving myself letting myself (with reasonable safely) be young and stupid? I've always wanted to be young and wise.

Me—To believe that you are on a holy journey to rediscover your own divinity and yet to feel as though you have been fucked by life is the epitome of dichotomy. For most of my life, my reality was limited to what my five senses told me. While there were moments of great happiness, there were also moments of hurt, disappointment, betrayal, turmoil, rage, and confusion. With the accumulated weight of these experiences, I questioned who I really was. Was this all there is? Is there nothing more? With despair came loneliness. And having yearned for something more, I reached out. As awareness began to grow, the lessons became more difficult and the yearnings more defined. And then a moment that is nearly impossible to define arrived. In that moment I turned to seek Light. Without any clear understanding of why, in that moment, it happened, there was the beginning of belief. It was also the beginning of a feeling of Oneness, with my fellow beings—souls incarnate, with all living things, with all nature, and with the very Earth itself.

CHAPTER 1

IN THE BEGINNING

I had, for more than fifty years of life, believed my mind. My five senses brought me all the information my mind needed to integrate the facts. My intellect would then take the facts and provide me with the blueprint of the reality of life and my role in that reality. I would be a doctor. My parents agreed that was indeed a fine profession to choose. I would do "good" and have a very comfortable existence. I would be a "success", a great catch for anyone looking to reel in a young successful doctor. I would be loved and admired. I would find happiness. And what would make me happy? To lead a long life. To have a nice roof over my head, good food on the table. Money of course—a goodly amount. A comfortable life. Good friends and family. A loving, adoring partner for life. Travel, leisure time. Respect. Some power maybe?—To do good things of course. To be a nice-sized fish in whatever pond I found myself in.

I have always had a great intellectual curiosity about Man and his universe. The big questions of the meaning and purpose of life have always been with me in some subliminal manner, but the easier questions of life and death seemed more within my grasp. Perhaps that is part of the reason I became a physician. So, over many years, I have become very well acquainted with both the mode of entry to and exit from this life. When it came to religious dogma and faith in a higher power, I completely recoiled in disbelief. To choose belief was not a choice I could make. Religions all seemed so disconnected to any truth I could imagine. Unless science could prove the existence of God, it was all silly nonsense: fairy tales for young and old of feeble minds. Prejudice was cloaked in religious garb, dividing, persecuting, and killing people, all in the name of God. What kind of God would allow it? That was all I needed to know about religion. I removed myself from such idiocy.

But life had other things in store for me.

It was a cold February night in 1994. Brent, my long-term lover, lay dying in his bed. There was a high snow outside his window, where bitter wintry air was blowing up a tempest, as if to set the stage for what was to come. In the stillness of his room, it was warm and intimate. The only sounds were our voices. I thought back to how and when our lives intersected and intertwined into one. A chance meeting and then a simple goodnight kiss the night I drove him home. We kept that one simple kiss going until I was so consumed with passion, I could think of nothing else but... But, we didn't for the longest time. By that time, we were head over heels in love—how amazing.

Now, I was too close to it all. I was his doctor as well as his lover. His faith and his trust in me had been his lifeline. I had no choice in that. Whether I felt burdened or not, I had long ago vowed never to abandon him or betray his trust. So, when I made the diagnosis of AIDS for Brent's long-apparent illness, I railed against the fates and cursed the God I refused to believe in.

I became an HIV specialist, treating and caring for Brent, along with many other friends.

Brent had always enjoyed that special charisma that would draw all eyes towards him. Strangers always imagined they knew him from somewhere. With his charming smile, larger-than-life personality, and wonderful heart, he was indeed beloved. He was "good" his entire life. He gave money to the homeless. He loved animals. His only enemy, fate, was most cruel.

His dream of making his Broadway stage debut was about to become a reality. His audition was flawless and he had his first major talent agent. But that promised Broadway debut was not to be realized.

His pain became my pain; his suffering became my suffering. I had no choice and in the end, I had no power. I could not save him. He asked me, "Why, for the love of God, did this happen to me? All my hope and belief in the future… It was only an illusion." I had no answer to offer back.

And so, this extraordinary and special young man, facing his own mortality so prematurely in a world transformed by AIDS, told me about belief. He knew he was to die that night. Talking about the possibility of an afterlife, he said he believed the next life would be better than this one. And I asked "Why?" What made him sure? His answer was simply because he chose to. Since belief was his choice, he would believe in something that made him happy. And a greater reality than the life we knew, with bliss yet to come, gave him comfort and brought him strength. Between hysterical sobs, I begged him to give me a sign if at all possible, any sign that he was right, that there was more to life beyond death. He nodded his assent. Then he said, "Someday, you'll meet a man again, who will give you his heart. I want you to give him this ring as a gift from me, a remembrance from the happiest days of my life." He took the ring from his finger and placed it in my hand. And I said, "There will never be another."

As death robbed him of his life, I helplessly watched his body convulse through all its fits and starts. Then, when the death rattle heralded the inevitable conclusion of his struggle, he took his very last gulp of air.

And in my arms, he died.

I had blinked and ten years had passed and it was finished. I was forced to realize that nothing lasts forever—the glorious dream of a lifetime of blissful happiness together had ended.

In the quiet of that room, I held him, caressed him and kissed him, for one final moment. I imagined I could feel his soul depart, as his body became cold and lifeless. I screamed with a fury to reach the heavens—a horrific blood-curdling noise, of anguish and pain. And then, I cried my heart out until I had no tears left to cry.

The next morning, I was standing in the shower, when suddenly, the water that was hitting my back seemed to stop. I turned around and saw the showerhead spinning clockwise with the inner plastic piece spinning counter-clockwise. Interrupting my sorrow, I instinctively screamed out, "Brent, is that my sign?!" That might have been the very first time I experienced profound joy and sadness all at once. My heart leapt for joy as my mind knew only sorrow. I reached up to stop the spinning, which it did as soon as I grabbed the showerhead. Having calmed myself, my rational brain took over and determined it was a problem with water pressure, or something like that. I then tried to reproduce my miracle by playing with the showerhead for the next half-hour, with no success. I was unable to recreate that magical moment—the fleeting feeling that there was something more beyond death. Although such an event had not happened before, and has not since in the twenty years I lived there, or anywhere else for that matter, I still did not quite embrace the mini-miracle of the spinning showerhead until a decade later.

Brent's passing was my second close encounter with death. Although as a doctor, I had seen death many times before, it was never this up-close and personal. With Brent, it smacked me in the face with a vague familiarity for which I was unprepared. That familiarity was born of my first close, personal encounter with death. It was intense and life-altering and different.

It was that of my grandmother, when I was fifteen years old. The intimacy and intensity, while no less profound, did not enter my home as did that frontal assault of Brent's illness and death. Her illness blindsided me and her suffering affected me greatly. She had cancer of the gallbladder, which caused her great pain. I watched as this vibrant woman wasted away, turning yellow and emaciated as death approached. At our last supper with her and our family, I insisted that we discuss the truth that she already knew. Everyone else tried to hide it from her, offering her pabulum instead. And then she told the assembled that I indeed did speak for her. She wanted a connection of truth with her loved ones and her condition. That was the last time I saw her alive.

Part of the human condition for anyone with the mental capacities to look beyond themselves and this life is, at some point, to confront personal mortality. In so doing, questions of fate, God, life's purpose, good and evil, the inevitability of death, and what lies beyond will ensnare and entangle every intellect. My grandmother's cancer and subsequent death was that moment for me.

While these may not be topics that fascinate everyone, they eventually will force themselves into every mind and hold each captive for some variable period of time. They will demand full attention and attention will be paid.

Whether it is the loss of loved ones, serious illness, some inexplicable cruelty, or one's own impending death, the mind will grapple with all these thoughts.

That final evening together, undoubtedly played a significant part in my decision to become a physician. I would offer comfort and understanding to those who suffer and do battle with illness and death.

So I became a physician—a noble profession. I became a specialist in internal medicine, the closest thing to a "healer" that I could envision. But then came drastic changes in health delivery, HMOs and managed care, malpractice suits, and insurance woes. My successful life was becoming much more difficult. And the periods of unhappiness that would come my way only multiplied as the stresses of the private practice of medicine increased.

I went into the restaurant business with a close friend to find the money, happiness, and success that was slipping away from my life as a doctor. Our restaurant was on Columbus Avenue, on the Upper West Side of Manhattan, a block from Central Park. We were immensely successful right from the start. The line to enter would wind around the block, down to the Park. Wearing two hats, I was still a doctor by day, but a restaurateur by night. It was while wearing that evening hat that I met Brent, just as the plague of my generation was showing its face to the world. He was the actor, singer, dancer, who came to work as a waiter in our restaurant, and all the while stole my heart. And so, it began. Enamored as we would become, it was only a matter of time until we would share our love and our lives under the same roof.

Then one night, the phone rang. There had been a fire at the restaurant. Brent and I raced up there. We walked through the charred ruins of my beautiful fifteen minutes of fame in numbed disbelief. It was gone. I lost all my money as I wound up in court with my friend/business partner as adversary. And I discovered that friends, if you do not know them well, and sometimes even if you do, might just have a very different view of friendship. Control, the scent of money, and rights to the future potential of our company name were the motives for the mutiny on the "ship of friend". The fire had been deliberately set. The Fire Marshall said it was an inside job. Betrayal of trust is an absolute minefield to cross. Trying to make sense of it is a story unto itself. Life continued to unravel.

Brent would die in just ten short years from the time we met.

Unbearable sorrow invaded my unhappy home. Someone changed my blueprint as a scourge hit the world. Fragments of thought swirled in my head as confusion reigned. Successful life? Fleeting moments of happiness in times of despair. A new reality to life! God? That would be farcical.

I then developed a series of failed relationships with good people whose dreams just collided with mine. In the midst of them all was one crazy young man who was abusive. And so I lay on the floor of the hallway of our building, bleeding from the arm he had ripped with his teeth as I saved my dog from his hands encircling her neck. As he threatened to kill her, a voice in my head said, "This is not my life." The poodle, Coco, was saved. He went to jail.

Thanks to laws designed to protect all parties, as he then falsely claimed abuse, I also found myself in jail. This simply could not be my life. Where was that lovely blueprint I once had? Yet, that awful experience would be only the first of two such temporary moments of insanity in the reality of my life.

But first, Brent's prediction would come true. As the embers of love were rekindled into a roaring inferno, Brent's ring fulfilled its new purpose, as a gift of remembrance and love.

CHAPTER 2

A WHIRLWIND OF PASSION

I fell in love with a certain painting, at the same moment, with the same feelings and the same understanding as Michael, as our thoughts magically intertwined in a Parisian gallery.

I look at that picture and it reminds me of why we were bound to one another in that moment. In the painting, two simians were traveling together. The younger was held on the shoulder of the older while playfully grabbing his tail. The "slightly older" ape shows a gentle wisdom and the younger chimp an impish delight. They are bound not only by physical closeness but a simian understanding and delight in life. The vivid colors gave it energy, a force that jumps off the canvas and says *That's Love.*

We had an innate understanding of one another. There were many similarities in our life situations, our outlooks, and in the structure of our friendships. We also had great harmony. We clicked. Michael got me. I got him. It was amazing to me. The intuitive understanding that we shared convinced me that we were soul-mates. When he took me on a birthday trip to Paris, I was overwhelmed by his largess. And I was charmed. And I fell head over heels in love. It was the first time I felt love in that way—swept off my feet in a whirlwind of passion, in the most romantic city in the world. I felt so very special; I felt so lucky to be loved so very much. I believed it to be "true love", as if any love might not be true. It seemed to echo a truism: you only know it when you know it.

The words in songs about love seemed to have new meaning for me. Poems about love now seemed to resonate with a newfound understanding. I gave him the ring which I had treasured most dearly, closely held in my heart, and during the previous ten years, safely kept in my home. He accepted it and much like Cinderella's glass slipper, it was a perfect fit. Happiness was assured. We would spend our lives together, forever!

But life had other things in store for me.

CHAPTER 3

TRANSFORMATIVE MOMENTS

The second moment of temporary insanity in the reality of my life was being in the wrong place, at the wrong time, dancing and chatting with the wrong person, on the wrong dance floor. As he was targeted and then arrested, I was swept along, leading to a twenty-four hour stay in a hell hole called "The Tombs" in lower Manhattan. This notorious place, a freezing cold, rat-infested jail, is properly known as the Manhattan Detention Complex. There was nothing to eat. The peanut butter sandwich they provided was inedible. It was two hard pieces of bread, with the thinnest imaginable daub of stale peanut butter. I took one bite and threw it away. I was unable or unwilling to use the toilet facility. Strategically placed off-center in the room, there sat a stainless steel toilet without seat. It was open to public view and covered with a splatter of excrement. Toilet paper required delicate negotiations with the jailhouse guards. They seemed willing to provide a single sheet or two, if you were willing to submit to a certain amount of verbal abuse. It was there in that hell-hole, surrounded by some twenty to thirty of the most potentially violent criminals rounded up that night, that I hit rock bottom. I imagined losing everything, my home, friends, family, and profession. I wrapped my arms around myself in an attempt to keep the cold at bay, as I rocked back and forth in childlike fashion. My entire life flashed before me, as I imagined it might at the moment of death. Was this the successful life I was promised? Who made that promise anyway? Happiness? I could not remember that word. Ah, *despair.* That's the word.

But thankfully, after several months of court appearances, worry, and fear, all charges were dismissed. "Hallelujah," cried out Michael as we left the courtroom. And while not a national holiday, I celebrate yearly as for no other; Hallelujah Day it was—October thirteenth.

I was able to resume my life, grateful for all that I have, and happy just to be alive. I had been blind-sided by a series of life-altering events. Totally unexpected, completely unbelievable, transformative moments. The hard, cold facts of life appeared at my door. Uninvited, they forced their way in. No one warned me that my happy, successful life, my blueprint of reality, and my role in it could be so easily altered without my consent.

So, while sitting in "The Tombs," disbelieving the moment I found myself in, another moment played itself over and over in my head. With so much "alone" time at my disposal, I could not help but wonder about life, death, meaning, purpose, and God. And so from the recesses of my mind I recalled another happier time, one that I had long denied to myself. Denied because it took my reality and turned it upside down and inside out. But then again, that was where I found myself anyway.

And this is where my story really begins. Once upon a time...

CHAPTER 4

MAGIC JOURNEYS

It happened strangely enough on a dance floor called Arabian Nights, on the outskirts of Disney World. Normally, this is a huge equestrian facility. But, for three nights a year, it is transformed into a colossal dance floor. A wood floor is laid, state-of-the-art equipment is brought in, and thousands come to revel in the magic of the music and the space. The official name of these after-parties is Magic Journeys. There I was, alone in my moment, sharing it with Michael, and at the same time sharing it with thousands upon thousands of others in moments of their own.

I was dancing with Michael. My eyes were closed and our lips were locked in embrace. I opened my eyes to gaze into his and watched in incomprehensible amazement. His face had morphed into that of another. The lights and sounds of the club receded. Newly heightened senses of sound and color, and brilliant light surrounded us. I gazed up at him to see a halo over his head and the shimmer of brilliant, sparkling, white and silver stars all around. He spoke to me with a power and presence that felt awesome in its magnificence. In that moment of embrace, he told me that I was deeply loved. I heard those words and felt a shiver of truth course through my body, as I understood that what he meant was "by God". And in that moment, as love flowed through my spirit and filled the room, I felt as though I had been touched by the hand of God. Bliss, a word whose true meaning I never knew, was made known. His face then returned to that of my Michael. In the immediate aftermath of that singular experience, I felt that God had spoken to me through Michael's transformed countenance. I thought I had lost my mind. In the euphoric glow that enveloped me when I left the dance floor, I felt as though I was walking on air. On our way out, I asked Michael whether he had experienced anything remotely similar to my experience. I assumed that if your presence is supplanted by God, you must feel something. He did tell me that while I was busy conversing with God, he too had a uniquely magical moment of his own. He experienced a euphoric, unique, and extraordinary sense of interconnectedness with me—a strong and unique synchronicity—a feeling of boundaryless blending—a oneness.

There was not a shadow of doubt in my heart. Whether I had lost my mind or not, I needed to return to the site of my miracle and see if I could experience another connection to a greater reality. And so, the following night, we went back to the portal, back to the dance floor...

We began to dance as we always did. It seemed at first that I was speaking with Michael. But, in no time, my universe shifted. Once again the lights and sounds of the club receded. Newly heightened senses of sound and color, and brilliant light surrounded us. I gazed up at him to see a halo over his head and the shimmer of brilliant, sparkling, white and silver stars all around. It was Michael, but it was not Michael. Somehow I had left the dance floor behind as I started an ascent. The name of the event, "Magic Journeys," seemed more than appropriate. There I was, a being of shimmering light with another being of light, feeling the most blissful content I had ever known. You can imagine that with such a surreal experience, my natural thought was that I must have died on the dance floor and perhaps I was entering heaven. He answered me and told me that my time had not yet come. I had not died. At some moment in that evening, my greater consciousness left my body on a journey of its own. As it turned out, some lesser portion of my conscious body, of which I was scarcely aware, continued to dance with Michael. And thus began my journey up the staircase of awareness. While I danced with Michael, I was speaking with a higher consciousness with the knowledge of All-That-Is. It was as close to a burning bush as I imagine it could be. Since it is too cumbersome to keep referring to a "higher consciousness", let me call him Emmanuel, whose name, in Hebrew, means "God is with us." If He was not God Supreme, he certainly spoke for Him.

I asked Emmanuel, believing I was asking God, every question that popped into my head. I wanted to know what God thought of organized religions, the Pope, Muslim extremists, and abortion. I wanted to know if God had a sense of humor. Since it is not the purpose of this book to invite extraneous controversy, let me just say that He does have a sense of humor. The answers to the other questions must await another forum. And as we conversed, and my questions were answered, I was led up a staircase. It seemed literally to be a staircase where at each new level I was given an awareness of All–That–Is that explained everything I did not understand from the prior level. Each level revealed more vivid colors and more glorious sounds, where physicality was gradually reduced. In its place, a progressively more vibratory state of being took hold. And at each level, I would playfully hit my head with my hand, exclaiming to Emmanuel, "Now I get it!"

Of course, at each new level it became apparent that I really had not truly "gotten it". At the very summit, a tableau played out for me. It was a scene of a birth, which I took to be my own. Not really wanting to repeat third grade all over again, I asked if I had to come back to do it all again. Emmanuel told me that this time I did not have to, unless I wanted to. It was to be a graduation from school at the end of this life.

Then with the deepest and most profound loving compassion, He told me that my continuing life would not come without the pain of further loss and hurt. But this road could not be avoided. My relationship with Michael would not continue. And so for the second time in memory, I felt profound sadness and joy in the same instant. To touch the grace of a greater reality and lose another "love of my life" to the "reality" of life is a difficult moment. Perhaps that is why I took that moment, to ask what was/is the meaning and purpose of life? Although much was not retained in my memory from this entire evening of amazing revelation, I remember these two answers vividly. The purpose of life was answered, *It Is All About Love*. The meaning of life was answered, *We Are All One*.

Afterwards my greater consciousness returned "home", knowing in the moment that I had a conversation with God, knowing that my life was and would be forever changed.

The most intriguing and mystifying answer I received was *We Are All One*. That is because it spoke directly to the truth of my experience.

I say this because my first question to Michael was, "What did it mean?". Now normally, if anyone has a thought of their own, they must know why they thought it or what it meant to them. For me, it was as if those words were grafted into my brain, without the associated understanding of any meaning. Could it simply mean we all go through the same life experience? Was there another meaning? A better explanation?

CHAPTER 5

FINDING MY HEART

As foretold, it was to be a very emotionally difficult personal journey. Michael did leave me, a few months following the revelation. It was as though a light switch had been flipped. One morning, he came upstairs and announced that he no longer wanted a romantic relationship. It was over and I was heartbroken, lost, and confused. This portion of the revelation I had, until then, kept to myself. And although this had been foretold, nothing could have or would have prepared me for the outcome. And nothing could have or would have changed the outcome. The ending of our relationship was heart-wrenching and excruciatingly painful.

This crossing of the minefield, strewn with feelings of hurt and betrayal, would wind up as a milestone breakthrough experience in my life's story. In the moment, though, all I could do was find my traumatized heart and let it heal.

Over the next couple of years I did often return in thought to my conversations with Emmanuel, determined not to forget, deny, or simply misplace my memory. This time, though, it is impossible to forget.

The awful times have receded in my memory. Hallelujah Day has passed. Two years later, I am visiting my dear friend Steven. It was into his eyes that I gazed, when Michael's face transformed, while on the dance floor of Arabian Nights. He is a very spiritual man: a Buddhist, and Reiki master. Although he was also on that Disney World vacation, he was not out with us that night. While Steven, as a Reiki master, can channel healing energy, that night was a "star turn".

I am at the library in his home in California. He is out walking his dog. I glance over the shelves of this large collection of eclectic books, when I am drawn by some mysterious force to a small book on the lower left hand shelf. I pull it from the shelf. It is entitled "Emmanuel's Book." It is the collected answers to life questions from a higher consciousness named Emmanuel. I open it. The first page I gaze at almost screams the words as the letters jump up at me, *We are all one.* The apparent coincidence is both another moment of grace and a confirmation that there is no such thing as coincidence. I know the truth of it and this time I choose to fully believe it and embrace it. I had found my heart. The pieces of the puzzle began to fall into place, as all the cumulative events of my life began to make sense to me. To finally find true love and compassion for self was a magical beginning to an eternal story. I was no longer compelled to look to another to verify my self-worth.

And the purpose of life was answered, *It Is All About Love.*

I went to a wake to be there for a close friend of long standing. His dear mother had died suddenly, albeit after many recurrent trips to the hospital. There had been some estrangement between us for the few years since he had begun dating my ex-lover Michael, eventually becoming his new lover. The wisdom of quieting the emotional outbursts of my mind, of allowing my heart and soul to align, had not yet been fully realized. So I was still filled with a "How could you?! You call yourself a friend?! What a selfish little fucker!" mindset.

Initially, the rational part of my brain went into overdrive trying to decide if I should go or not. There were layers of hurts and disappointments that, if allowed, could encrust my heart forever. The best any human being can strive for is imperfect perfection. So, I acknowledge those emotions of my mind, while reaching for the true feelings of my heart. Thankfully, I have now reached that moment in life when I can give decision making over to my heart and ask my mind to take a back seat. There is love and magic to found everywhere. The best moment is that moment of NOW. And so it was, and so it is. My heart shared and offered love and love was received and returned.

As I wrote the sympathy card I thought of the heartfelt lyrics to the John Lennon song, *All You Need Is Love*. My words came from my heart. "While you have come to that moment of loss that ultimately is that common thread that is woven into the lives of all humanity— one that I share, without your full knowing of such a loss (for my moment yet awaits)—Know that the bounds and bonds of love transcend time and space and last for eternity plus half a second."

When I first heard the words, *It Is All About Love*, their meaning seemed fairly simple and straightforward. With the benefit of the illusion of time, I can now say this simple statement can be thought of in the most profound terms. On the simplest level, *It Is All About Love* is the golden rule. Treat others as you would wish to be treated; love your neighbor as yourself. On a deeper level, it is the nature of our life experience, which is testing the boundaries and limits of self-love, love of others, and love of God, which incorporates any relationship you can imagine, including denial of all the above.

To experience love where love must leave itself to find itself is a most challenging and difficult curriculum. But that curriculum connects directly to a greater reality and All-That-Is.

So now, songs about love and poems about love have an even greater beauty for me. I bring an even greater understanding from a higher (not better) level of awareness. And so it continues to go and so it shall always go throughout eternity.

And I am so grateful in so many ways. For all of the loves of my life, and all the pain and suffering, for all the "true love" and the "false" starts, for the momentary bliss, for the enduring special friendships that continue unwavering in nature and steadfast in strength, and for the angelic heart that I know is at everyone's core, I now offer back my eternal love, knowing that all love is true. With great compassion for the curriculum of others, I will shine my light where they may yet find darkness.

I have discovered that my greatest strength is born from love. To recognize "true" love is not always easy. Sex can confuse even the brightest intellect, from common man to president.

Ken, identified in the dedication of this book, said someone could stab me in the heart and I would let it heal and then forgive them.

I think he knows me well. For I have found that love of self and compassion for self that allows me to have the same for others.

A gift should be freely given. So Michael remains connected to Brent through the remembrance. The ring was his to choose and keep. And he did and it is love.

CHAPTER 6

AT THE SPEED OF TIME

I think that looking back to my childhood, I never really felt the force of my personality was sufficient in the arena of interpersonal relationships to charm and hold forth in life. It is a familiar story of gay youth. Certainly, coming of age in the 1950's and 60's, this was the obvious bogeyman to blame for my lack of self-esteem.

The end result was a need to impress people, and that came in the form of largess. I was the fabulous young doctor with the fabulous large apartment, fabulous artwork, fabulous trips, and fabulous extravagances of all kinds... all to catapult my charms to the fore. And it worked very well. Doctor Monkey (my nickname) was very popular. But also a bit self-absorbed and self-centered, and some might say a bit selfish. Certainly a bit materialistic.

It was easy to give material things to those I cared about. It was much more difficult to give of myself. The need to lead my own life as I wish was my mantra. One of the benefits of being gay, I thought, was a certain lack of accountability and responsibility to others. It was recompense for the difficulties that being gay could bring. Part of the rights and privileges earned for a more difficult journey. Without a family to raise or a spouse to consider, it seemed natural. Over the course of time though, it has taken me away from many who I have loved or have loved me. Despite being a "good person", I have done things that have caused emotional hurt and pain to others along the way. It was never by intent or by design. But it was in that self-centered pursuit of a formerly elusive goal. For those moments, I do have true remorse. It is part of the beauty of my human imperfection. And the most I can hope for is that perfect imperfection. Perfection is not a goal for this life. Love and compassion, however, are achievable.

So, my life's trajectory has brought me to the perfect moment, which I now truly realize as the only moment.

My role as a gay man is simply my role. It is my human costume. It is the one I chose pre-birth when my soul consciousness decided to explore love in denser matter.

It neither adds to nor detracts from truth. For some, it may only speak to one's level of awareness, one's love of self and one's ability to have love and compassion for the journey of others.

As I travelled from Fire Island to Manhattan, writing part of this story, I turned on my iPod. The title announced, "Journey—Don't Stop Believing." I set my pen down to reflect and think, as random shuffle next brings me "Kinda New." The words—"We all live and die."

Messages from the universe, from All-That-Is, can come in all forms. Since I do not believe in coincidence, I bring my own perspective to these "random" events.

There are personal demons that we all carry with us: the lack of self-worth in some particular area; perhaps a more generalized low self-esteem; commonalities we all bring to the life experience. At the outset, disconnected from All-That-Is, there is always a sense of isolation; always a sense of inferiority, simple or complex; suffering of one sort or another. The fears that hinder lives also shape and mold them. We can let go of them or they can consume us. We all have crutches to get us through our fears and doubts. It can be alcohol, drugs, sex, gambling, apparent mental illness or any other choice that assuages our plight, lessens our hurt or takes the edge from our pain.

There are people, too, who truly demonize one's life. But they are not there by chance. It is part of the trajectory of one's curriculum. We all make choices variably based on love or the absence of love, more commonly referred to as "hate". It is through those choices that we can develop true self-love. This is a requisite part of the life experience. How many lifetimes may this take? Clearly, it does not happen for anyone in this one life.

The ability of my story to resonate has to do not with the human costume I wear, nor the role I play, but to the strength of connection to a greater reality we all share; a truth felt in our hearts that may not yet be known.

We are cast by choice in the roles of our distinct personalities—to play that human being with a script that has pages that only last for a part of each act at any one time. The remaining pages are then only rushed into our hands as they roll off the presses, and we, as the contract players we are, handle these unexpected twists and turns with compelling skill, so all might believe that this illusion is real.

The trick is in straddling the physical and spiritual and making sense of both, remaining grounded in the reality we live and aware of the greater reality that connects us to truth. Somewhere along the journey between live (life) and die, moments of grace can be distilled from a greater reality. Realize, in physicality, that while we are subject to the forces that govern this world, we can still recognize a purpose and meaning that transcends those forces.

It is ultimately better to face reality if one can recognize it. If one is drowning under a mound of debt, it is better to confront that reality with sound debt restructuring than to be forced from one's home and stripped of one's possessions.

It is so much easier to put off those inconvenient questions that can interfere with the "business of living" than to face them early in life. I had an anatomy professor in medical school who used to say what the mind does not know the eye cannot see. So expand your mind so you can know truth and see how to embrace it.

There is a fabric and texture that is woven into a pattern—the interconnectedness of one's life with all those who have played significant parts. This pattern seems more apparent, and may even be understood through the looking glass of greater reality. If knowledge is power, then this can empower.

We all have within us a spiritual essence which has the capacity for growth and enlightenment that can transcend our earthly bounds.

The gift of life allows for this. Imagine, if as children, we were all taught this truth. It is at such a tender and impressionable age that we have the capacity to feel as one with the universe more easily. This spiritual connection to All-That-Is has little in common with religion. Although we may all have the same final destination, this life is a singularly personal journey, as is my story. But my story can offer comfort on the journey for those who can embrace it.

Time can move quickly and slowly at the same speed, all at once and not at all, for it is illusion. And within that illusion there are moments in (no) time.

A wise person once told me that there is what you know you know, what you know you don't know, and what you don't know you don't know. To put a slightly different spin on it, I have found there is what I know I know (from direct personal knowledge), what I think I know (from what I surmise based upon what I know), and what I know I don't know.

To take this one step further, we should choose to believe in something that truly resonates with our spiritual essence—that individual energy that has been called the "soul". When belief so resonates within us, the perfect harmony we experience means we feel truth. That is the first step. To feel it is to know it. That which the heart knows, we can begin to believe.

So, I know there is a greater reality within a world of spirit or higher consciousness. I know that the world of spirit can communicate with us and I know that communal consciousness binds us, most especially through music and other art forms. I know there is God and that we are eternal; I know it is all about love; I know we are all one.

There is a common behavioral response known in psychiatric terms as maladaptive behavior. Essentially you know, at some level, what you want, but the choices you make to attain it are so counter-productive that your chances of reaching your goal are slim. It is more likely that you would even wind up with its opposite.

With greater understanding, we may choose more wisely at the many forks in our life's road. And if not more wisely, at least acknowledging that we are at a pivotal moment of choosing. Which road leads to "Love"? Are we choosing "Love"? Are we choosing "truth"? Those are questions all should ask.

CHAPTER 7

QUANTUM LEAP

Science has made huge leaps in understanding our world and universe, in areas such as physics, biology, and astronomy. The time for a quantum leap in "religious" thought and understanding is long past due. God-Consciousness needs to replace religious distortions; personal introspection needs to replace warped dogma.

Throughout recorded history, when man did not understand his world, he often chose to invoke a magical explanation and then deify it.

Either we take the truth and shroud it in religious nebula, mystification, and confusion, or we imagine that it does not exist. Eventually, religion distorts truth, until it needs to be fed and sustained for its own growth and its own sake. Shorn of the encrustations and deformations that have nearly destroyed truth, spiritual enlightenment will flourish on this planet.

Truth melds seamlessly with science, as it must, because it enfolds it. As we recognize truth for what it is, there is an interlocking of spirituality and science. As truth is understood, straw-man dichotomies between evolution and creationism fade away. How can we reconcile all the inconsistencies of life as we know it when we invoke magical explanations that explain nothing?

There is a universal theory of everything. And in that truth exist the answers we seek. Truth encompasses and embraces science because everything emanates from the same wellspring of reality.

There is a physical principle, as we know it and live it on our planet. Two objects cannot occupy the same space at the same time. Likewise, two truths cannot exist simultaneously. This refers to truth with a capital "T" and that rhymes with "G" and that stands for God. It is an inviolate constant principle of the universe. There is and can be only one truth. People may have different experiences and understandings of truth. But those shades of gray do not alter truth.

Whether one brings a simple understanding or a physicist's post-graduate training to the force called gravity, gravity is still the same. The attraction between objects based on mass may appear different on the moon's surface as compared to the earth's, but the force itself is the same. Likewise, truth is unchangeable and unwavering in its consistency. Since there can be only one truth, it follows that "they" all cannot have it right. "They" are the well-recognized major religions, their many offshoots, and a host of idiosyncratic belief systems. Does only one have it right? Are they all wrong? Or are there bits and pieces of truth in each—covered over, with so much overlaying, ritualistic, self-sustaining bloat, that to catch a glimmer of truth requires going back to the future?

With the sharing of my story, it now comes time to share truth as fully as I know it to be. truth contains an understanding of that word— "God". And it is with great humility and without any arrogance that I say this. No one can verify this truth, neither for me nor for you. And no one needs to do so.

So, if you have read this far, it is fair to connect the dots…

And the meaning of life was answered, *We Are All One*. The understanding of this can take many lifetimes to grasp and believe. And depending on the level of awareness you have, the answer can sound like gibberish or profound truth. Many, many, books have been written on this topic and it is not my desire to simply add another. I offer an explanation to satisfy those who are able to embrace it.

We Are All One refers not to the human costumes we wear, but to our souls, or soul consciousness. When the universal consciousness of All-That-Is decided to explore love moving in denser matter, we as individuating consciousness separated from the Oneness. I have been alive for eternity plus half a second, as have we all. Not in this body or as this personality of course, but my soul consciousness as part of All-That-Is.

Each soul consciousness is a part of God, dusted with physicality, wearing the human costume, attending school in a classroom called Earth. Being alive for eternity plus half a second, I (as have we all) come to this classroom called Earth by choice. For it is only in this physicality that my soul consciousness can grow in certain ways. The human condition is one of duality intrinsic to our being. It is angel and human and the choices we make in our dual roles.

The first major achievement in growth is attaining love of self and compassion for self. Then can come love of others and compassion for others. This also means allowing others their journey, as no one of us can change another, although our influence or presence clearly can play a significant part.

Ultimately comes love of God, which completes the process of exploration in physicality, of the limits and boundaries of love. Beyond those boundaries of physicality comes the willing choice to give oneself over to serve God, which means to serve Love. This is a spiritual and not physical concept, a free choice of your higher consciousness that can occur once the negativity that was requisite for the life experience has been resolved.

On the very deepest level, Love is the most powerful force that exists, as a creative energy that has manifested our universe, transcending space and time—indeed, creating them. God is Love.

Exploration at the leading edge of creativity is what we are about. Oneness can never truly fragment, so the illusion of multiplicity belies the truth, *We Are All One.* If this makes sense to you, great! If not, I offer up: "At least there is an answer." It certainly gives more heft to the thought that every conversation we ever have is a conversation with ourselves.

So, now armed with the purpose and meaning of life, told to me by God, what do I do with this knowledge? I write a book. And give the barest minimum of advice.

Free your mind. Listen for the music, for it is indeed the message. You have got to believe in magic if you find it.

It is the heart that will open the door to Light and Truth—Understanding that It Is All About Love and Knowing that We Are All One—Appreciating its perfection—Believing that there is a God Supreme, and a universal soul consciousness of All-That-Is and that we, with our unique personalities and our individual soul consciousness, are a part of that divinity.

That soul consciousness is the angel we carry within us, no matter how far removed from Light and truth. Love is the creative force that forever will continue to create, as love must, for that is its very nature, for now & forever. Thus, Eternity.

CHAPTER 8

THE SCHOOL OF LIFE

I have come to believe that the school of life should be viewed as three distinct parts, for ease of understanding the nature of the experience.

One is acquisition of life skills. That is the mode by which you either make your way in life or fail to make your way, in terms of successful integration into society: making a living, making good friends, keeping good friends, finding the joy and happiness that this world can offer. In theory the more skills you possess, the more likely you are to have an easy life. But that premise may not necessarily be true. It is possible that may not be your curriculum. The hard, cold facts of life may come knocking at any time and invite themselves in to up-end your expertly-acquired skill set. So, the best advice in choosing which life skills to pursue is to follow your dreams and listen to your heart. Your mind is simply there to help navigate your way. Left unchecked, however, it has a way of assuming a position of authority about matters it knows nothing about.

Part two is the acquisition of wisdom. That is easy to explain but very difficult to achieve, because it only occurs through the process of living. But at least you can anticipate it. Wisdom is the knowledge to tell your mind to be quiet and your intellect to take a back seat so that your heart can lead. This will bring happiness.

Part three is achieving a measure of enlightenment. To touch the hem of the garment of a greater reality, not fully knowing how magnificent that garment truly is. "Grace"—knowing it is there through that fleeting touch, and satisfied without seeing it in all its brilliance. Moments of grace bring enlightenment, a connection to All-That-Is. As an understanding of oneness with a universal consciousness that connects to God and your true home becomes your reality, you find true peace and happiness. For it is then that you find love of self and compassion for the difficult road you have chosen to travel. And with that comes compassion and love for others. You can then be all that you really are—a Being of Light.

And having found out the truth of it all, to paraphrase Emmanuel, the dance of eternity can truly begin.

Each of us has our story. It is hard enough to begin to understand our own personal life's journey, which makes it nearly impossible to understand anyone else's journey. So the best one can do is allow. Allow all those you choose to love to follow their dreams so they may know their hearts. Recognize that no one is here to sacrifice their life or their dreams (even if they collide with yours) on the altar of love or friendship. You cannot look to people who do not yet know themselves in order to verify your self-worth, as they have yet to verify their own. The empty gestures of giving when there is nothing to give, or professing love when there is not enough love for self, need to be seen in that context.

So what is the true measure of a successful life?

Your dreams are followed. Your heart is known.

It is important to clarify that these are your innermost dreams, those of your soul consciousness, as it begins to seek out Light. These are not the dreams of the mind, but of the heart. The dream is passionate, ardent, and heartfelt. When the mind starts interfering, by telling you what you must do, recognize that it is background noise. Should you find wisdom and enlightenment, you can shine your light where there is darkness. The soul consciousness that exists at the core of each of us is Angel, no matter how seemingly disconnected from Light and truth. We can all be thought of as fallen angels. To find the angel within requires turning one's gaze inward. It is within our humanity that we can discover divinity. When you are overflowing with compassion and love for self, you can truly offer compassion and the most generous love to others. If you discover the angel within and know you are eternal, you are on the way home.

Realizing all of this in no way compromises the compelling drama of life. It is crafted too well. You will not give up on life. You will still strive and yearn and love and lose and make mistakes. You will still hunger for success. You are human, after all.

EPILOGUE

WELCOME TO A GREATER REALITY...

Since I have started sharing my own extraordinary experiences, people have felt comfortable sharing their stories with me. Friends and family, who never before have discussed these "things", now tell me of their own experience that comes to them from outside of the five senses we know. There is a singular commonality that is the binding of these collected tales. And that is that moment of grace wherein a greater reality is known.

I share five stories, in my own order of strength of communication from higher consciousness.

A patient of mine came for his regular visit. He had just returned from his first cruise ship vacation. He told me he had the most amazing experience. As he had a recent traumatic separation from his partner of 25 years, I assumed he had met someone. That was not it at all. During one of the big dance parties on the ship, he made his way to the bow, feeling drawn to it by a mysterious force. From that spot, he watched the sunset. It was a solitary moment—not another person was there. The music from the dance floor was inaudible as the blowing wind was all he heard. The beauty of that moment, watching the sky meet the setting sun on the ocean's horizon, moved him to uncontrollable tears. As he sobbed more for the joy of the moment than anything else, a breath of wind suddenly crossed both cheeks blowing his tears away. In that instant, he felt as though a huge weight had been lifted and from that moment he is a changed man. It is an amazing story of grace. It is also amazing to me that he offered to share it with me as more and more people have. Having touched the greater reality in my own life, I was able to share in his experience from a much better vantage point of understanding and total belief. It is difficult at first to discuss these experiences because the language of our everyday lives is not sufficient to describe these moments of spirit. But, as one learns a new language, a new vocabulary can be developed to communicate matters of the heart.

A very close friend lost his mother several years ago. As it is with such a loss, there remains an emptiness that is extraordinarily difficult to overcome. With her death came nightly dreams, in which she would come to him, calling him by name and saying, "Son, you still don't understand." As you might imagine, after quite a few years of nightly dreams with the same scenario, one might well be very frustrated if not troubled by the mind's incomprehensible repetition. After several such years, he found himself in that stage of early awakening, still semi-asleep but with the stirrings of alertness setting in. At this moment, as his mother repeated her mantra, "Son, you still don't understand," he suddenly blurted out, "You're still with me!!" From that moment, fortified with that understanding or bit of wisdom of things greater, he has never had that dream again.

I was at a party where I met an acquaintance who told me of the time her life was saved in a more direct and physically-connected manner. As a young girl, she was in her car and driving to the local mall, just a few blocks away. Suddenly, a voice said to her "Put your seat belt on!" She ignored the voice at first, thinking she was having a mental conversation with herself, and reasoning that the mall was only a few blocks away and she did not need to follow this advice. Again the voice said more forcefully, "Put on your seatbelt!!" This time she complied, somewhat confused that the voice seemed outside her head. The light turned green in her favor and as she started through the next intersection a car ran the light in the other direction, slamming into her vehicle and wrapping itself around her car. Stating the obvious, she was saved from certain grievous injury and possible death. I add that she claims no psychic powers and has no other story to offer from the next twenty five or so years of her life—at least not yet.

My fourth story comes from another friend, who apparently never told anyone until he related it to me in a moment of shared experiences. In the winter of 1994 (coincidentally the winter of Brent's death), he was driving from Minneapolis to Madison, Wisconsin. Driving in the upper Midwest at that time of year usually involves some snow and, as on this particular day, black ice, which as its name implies, blends with the asphalt so you cannot distinguish it from the road. He is halfway through his trip, with only a lone Pontiac Firebird on the road ahead of him. And then it happens. The Firebird hits the brakes. My friend knows with a certainty that the Firebird was going to spin out of control. Given the road conditions, there was no way he would avoid slamming into it. And sure enough, the car in front fishtails, starts to tailspin, and then spins out right in front of him. My friend, braking his car the best he could under the icy road conditions, was still about to hit the other car. From that point it all seemed to go in slow motion for him. He could see himself approaching the spinning Firebird, frame-by-frame, as though in a movie. He came within about one-half inch of that near fatal moment. Just as he was about to plow into the back side/end of the car, he saw a large hand (about two to three times the size of his Honda Civic) reach down on top of his car. The hand was white, yet translucent, and giving off a blue-tinged glow. Within that frame, his physical ability to react was lost to the moment. He could only anticipate the inevitable end. In that nanosecond, that surreal hand somehow jerked his car sideways onto the median (which was nothing but a grassy ditch covered in half a foot of snow). The Firebird wound up on the opposite side of the highway. My friend was able to pull his car out of the ditch and back on the road in a few minutes. And now, fifteen years later, the vision of that hand remains as vivid and clear as day it happened.

My last story was only just recently shared with me by my editor. A number of years ago, he had been up quite late at a friend's house. Before heading home, he took a nap. Having just gotten his driver's license, it was not surprising that he would dream he was in his car. In that dream, he was driving down a wide street late at night. Just as he was about to enter the intersection, he saw a stop sign nearly obscured by a low hanging tree branch. "Well it's really late and I don't see any other cars. I'm just going to blow through the intersection," he thought to himself. As he sped through the intersection, off to his right, a white sedan, with its headlights off, lurched in front of him. He slammed into the sedan, T-boning the driver's side, knowing that both he and the other driver were severely injured, if even alive. At that moment, he woke with a start and then recounted the dream to his friend. She said to be careful driving and he left.

On the way home he took a detour to go sit by the river near where he used to live. As he drove down the street that he used to walk down, he recognized the intersection from his dream—complete with a low hanging branch in front of the stop sign! Initially, he had the same thought as in his dream. "Well it's really late and I don't see any other cars. I'm just going to blow through the intersection." In the split second as recognition of the reality of his dream hit him, he slammed on the brakes. Not another soul was to be seen. As he came screeching to a halt, that same white sedan flew through the intersection from his right! Had it not been for his prophetic precognitive dream, he would not have stopped. Certainly limb, if not life, was spared.

So, let your mind run wild. Imagine you are he and that you had one singular experience that defied any "normal" explanation. Where would you place that experience? Would you run to the office and fearlessly share it with one and all? Would you hide it in the recesses of your mind? Forget it ever happened?

How does the rational mind explain these occurrences? In the first story, the easy explanation is that in his grief and loneliness, the chance gust of wind was given a meaning of his own invention. Then, feeling "special", he felt better about himself.

In the second story, the easy explanation is that in his grief his mind just played tricks on him, until he finally let time pass and grief subside.

The third story is a bit more difficult to rationalize. She might simply have had a thought that she debated in her head. Then, by a quirk of fate, her more cautious self won the argument, which coincidentally saved her from a possibly fatal accident. The fact that she actually heard a voice outside her head is put on the back shelf to be ignored, since the trauma of the event clouded her recollection.

For the fourth story, knowing that he is grounded in the same reality that we normally live, clearly he must have been falling asleep at the wheel. He did not realize that he was hypnotized by the snowy expanse and the constant beat of the windshield wipers. When he suddenly woke to avoid a collision, his mind played tricks on him as he was still not in his right head.

The last story nails it. There is no other plausible explanation but the truth.

Now with anything that comes into our lives from a greater reality, there is a natural tendency of the mind to try to explain, in the context of what we understand, the things that we have glimpsed. Find a "natural", "scientific", "reasonable" explanation, says the mind! Otherwise, you must ignore such an occurrence or people will view you and your views with suspicion. Moreover, these experiences with greater reality are topics that must be avoided in normal social situations for fear of abject ridicule. For most of us, even beyond the fear of rejection and humiliation, we are simply ill-prepared to deal with the "big-picture" issues of life—the meaning and purpose, and the mode of entry and exit from it.

Having fully embraced the truth of my own experiences with a greater reality, I take each story on the face of it. Each has connected with a greater reality as well. There can be much comfort found in the sharing of these experiences, as these resonant truths allow those who can to more easily know their own hearts. It is that which is so freeing—to let truth replace fear.

FORGETTING
AND
REMEMBERANCE

—A STORY BEYOND TIME

Howard Lawrence Scheiner, MD/AAHIVS

"AFTERWORDS"

A PROLOGUE

I made a leap of faith and as a result achieved a sense of freedom that I have never before experienced. That leap was to believe the reality I experienced and not to doubt the truth of what happened. If God tells you the meaning and purpose of life, it leaves you a changed person. My "burning bush" moment left me a changed person—I knew bliss.

I do not claim any special powers or abilities. Who I AM speaks only to a level of awareness. I do find myself in the mold of others from the historical past; I am connected (spiritually) to a greater reality.

Even with this new level of awareness, I can still find myself trapped in a nexus of disillusionment and disappointment, displaced from the moment—a part of being human.

Yet that fleeting moment of knowing, having felt the touch of God upon my soul, allows me to enter the state of Grace which I now touch every day.

None of this will negate the potential ambushes that can overtake one's life in a flash, no matter which road is chosen. Nor is it any sort of guarantee of wealth, health, social status, or the usual measures of success.

This book is not "The Secret." The true "secret" is there is no "secret", only a "truth".

"FORWARD"

A LOOK BACK

With greater understanding came a new perspective. "a Book of Life-Welcome to a Greater Reality," was and is the story of my personal journey to understanding and belief in a Greater Reality.

The words I now write come from this new and different perspective—words that come to me outside and beyond my five senses. They come from spirit; from my greater wisdom and my expanded consciousness. They come with the yielding to and the certainty in my fundamental trust. Trust that I am held in the hands of Perfect Love; of All-That-Is. It is with great humility that I write this book. Far from believing that I have reached any pinnacle of understanding, I believe that I have simply glimpsed a light through a door that is opened but a crack. But to reach that door and throw it wide open will take at least the rest of this life. And I have no doubt, that I will stumble many more times on the path to that door.

It seems that so often, the same set of circumstances seem to present themselves on a well worn path to "choice". And at the moment of choosing, voices of fear and doubt make themselves known. If those voices overpower one's heart, usually one chooses exactly as one has always chosen. If those voices suddenly become nearly inaudible, then one may choose differently than ever before—allowing one's heart to be heard. No matter how much I may want to dance on a rainbow as my consciousness is raised, there are always personal demons, set on pulling me back down from the heavens.

It is an ongoing truth of my life that habitual conformity, familiar distortions, and enduring confusions are the weighty luggage that I have carried for quite a while. All this baggage truly had weighed me down, imposing a great impediment to flying higher. Recognizing this, I constantly strive to lighten my consignment of luggage, by unburdening myself, whenever I can, of bags jam-packed with the fears of a lifetime. But doubt comes with being human, so at best I will always have a small carry-on.

So, it is a process, of purging the toxins of fear and doubt; listening to one's heart; finding a greater reality that allows for a new choice as consciousness grows. It is a process, of battling personal demons, small or large, and growing beyond them. It is a process of leaving the bags behind while ascending a ladder of awareness. So while I am comfortable with the awareness I presently have, I am not complacent.

I have purposely altered the true personalities and fictionalized the archetypal characters that follow. Forever lost with the particulars of their identities are the discarded memories of their family histories.

There is not one soul who incarnates into physicality without some sort of negativity, distortion, or confusion. These are the selected works of this lifetime. These are the areas we will explore through the experiences we bring to this life.

For the sake of clarity, I have distilled the primary negativities of my friends' chosen journeys—those distortions they have chosen to explore in this lifetime. These negativities are made obvious with the names I have chosen for my companions.

Each of us, for the purpose of this story and in this life, is portrayed with literary license, as an archetype for a specific variation of personality in the manner in which fear is chosen and love denied. To the extent that anyone sees any resemblance to themselves in these portrayals is only a matter of belief and identification with resonating distortion.

Belief can be altered at any moment...

With a new level of awareness of an ordered and loving universe, I write.

FORGETTING &
REMEMBRANCE

I am going to tell you a story of forgetting and remembrance. It is a story that you already know but have long forgotten. You must suspend disbelief in order to touch the memory. You can hear it in your heart, for that is where it will resonate. Your mind is too limited to understand it, so you must gently tell it to be still and let your heart soar, as it listens, and remembers a story born of love, filled with light, and knowing only truth. It is the story that tells you why you were born to die and yet will live forever. It is the story that provides a touchstone for all who believe that there must be more and who yearn for it. It is the story of how you came to be a human being, and what the true purpose and meaning of your life is. It is the story of time before time, and you and I are there. And it is the story without end when time is not. For as you will soon discover time is an illusion. It is a necessary tool, a device to keep us focused on life's events—nothing more.

For all who discover true resonance in the story of my journey, realize that I am simply stoking the embers of your remembering into the flames of reawakening. When you fully reawaken and remember the divinity that walks within your human costume, and the Oneness that we all are with All-That-Is, we will welcome one another home again, as we reconstruct the image of the self of our human adventure with the greater SELF, with the Oneness of all things and with GOD that we are. We are all ONE—one energy, one reality, one perception, one divinity, one God.

And so begins my timeless tale about love discovered, love betrayed, and love reborn—a journey home.

But let me not get ahead of myself. For long before that moment...

Once **upon a time**, before the illusion of time, we came as spirit into the presence of God. In a moment that is now impossible to recall, and in the consciousness that we were, we came in love to serve love. In the Oneness that we were, as it is our nature to create, we said we would go out into the void and create as we went. However many realities we touched at the leading edge of creation, we eventually identified with what we were creating and in the process became lost and disoriented from who we really are.

In order to remember and reawaken to our fundamental essence, we eventually decided to explore love where love is not, where God is not, and where we don't know who we really are. And that realm was where our spirit was dusted with physicality, in a world of duality—Earth. Everything on this planet affords choice. Choose light or darkness, good or evil, right or wrong, selfishness or selflessness, belief or disbelief, humanity or divinity—the list is endless. Contradictions and distractions of all sorts abound. It is here that we explore, as we choose what we believe in the moment.

Yet, while we have free choice along the way, the journey of the soul must be honored. There are boundaries that frame the journey, the blueprint of which cannot be changed.

Individual consciousness and collective consciousness have come together in this moment to manifest in the form of physically materialized matter. NOW is the moment in which eternity has chosen to take physical form. Our mutual creation is our mutual dream. When we leave this dream, we return to the primary reality, to All-That-Is, a wiser prodigal son through having experienced what we believe as a soul. Those experiences wear away layers of God denial thus adding to the reality of God. All things change as moments unfold and all consciousness continues to grow in awareness, even, I daresay, the consciousness of God.

Consciousness individuates as souls decide to incarnate in human form. We take on the personality that is the human being, and in so doing forget the divine origin of our spirit being. This is an essential part of the fragmentation. It allows life to be as compelling an illusion as it is. One could not immerse oneself in the full gamut of human experience if one did not believe fully in its importance and its reality.

Each soul chooses the degree of denial of Light that best suits its own needs as it experiences what it believes.

It is as if one is sitting in a room and choosing the lighting. In so choosing, one may limit the clarity with which one sees the interior and also the clarity with which one is seen. The choice of lighting may depend on the event of the moment. If one is having a liaison, perhaps a softer light which is less revealing is preferred. If there is a sexual encounter, perhaps one prefers total darkness. If joy takes hold on a sunlit day, perhaps all the blinds are pulled up and the windows thrown wide open.

And so, in life, there are degrees of denial of Light. There are clearly individuals whose lives seem to hold nothing but suffering. There are others whose lives seemed filled with joy. And between the two extremes are all the variations we see.

THE ROXY

Once upon a time, in the years following the plague of AIDS, there was a club called *The Roxy*. For nearly 20 years and spanning the turning of a millennium, it was the heart and soul of my life. On Eighteenth Street, off of the West Side Highway in New York City, was my Moulin Rouge. There, conveniently located within walking distance of my home, was the center of the universe. It was there that every trick, acquaintance, friend, lover, or spouse, shared the music, the dance, the euphoria, the drinks, the drugs, sex, and the nightlife. Over the span of that moment lovers came, lovers went, and lovers died. Friends grew together and friends grew apart. Magical moments, tragic moments, moments of sublime love immortal, and betrayals of those loves all played out on that stage.

The plague had unalterably changed the message and messenger in my life as it did for a generation. The innocence of youthful love was recast in a world turned upside-down. But it was at *The Roxy* that a once-in-a-lifetime tale was spun by fates, and angels, and devils within. It was there that I began to understand the higher purpose of my journey; it was there I glimpsed higher purpose in the journey of others. We all brought love, and sexuality, and hope with us in that timeless moment. But we also brought illness, addiction, abuse, loneliness, and betrayal.

The Roxy was magical. It was a microcosm which each week compressed into one evening the confusions, distortions, and truths we individually and collectively believed. And by the end of an evening, there was growth, personal and collective. It might have been infinitesimally unrecognizable in the moment, but it was there. And it was cumulative. After twenty years, the "me" that I recognized then has grown exponentially into the "me" I recognize now—yet I am the same unique individual.

So, how can one measure the growth of the heart—this organ which is the figurative, muscular representation of the strength and energy of love? When it is scrunched, compressed and constricted, the amount of love that can flow, in or out, is restricted as well. As it grows the energy of love flows more freely. But what words exist for the levels of growth beyond "big-hearted" and beyond that beyond? I recognize growth within my own consciousness and there are no words that adequately describe this growth of my heart—to more freely allow the full energy of love to flow unrestrained through unobstructed, non-convoluted, straight-forward channels.

And just to add another level to ponder—all moments, past, present, future, really are NOW. The "me" that I recognize now, with this larger heart, feels a new connection with my first lover who died in a moment that came far too prematurely. This connection grows despite the absence of his physical presence in this earthly realm. To discover that love can grow and connect beyond space and time adds to this reality of all moments being NOW. When we fully meet again in spirit, each will recognize the other, although we both will have grown separately and together, all at once.

What began for me as a way to celebrate life with my friends, in the wake of the onslaught of AIDS, became more than just a celebration. It was part of life's curriculum which is to learn through the gathering of all experience; the purpose of life—*It Is All About Love*. That is life's journey—growing in understanding, through the experiences we bring to ourselves—to come to a greater awareness of what *It Is All About Love* can mean.

That simple statement, which almost anyone can understand on its face value, is the very same eternal complexity that we spend lifetimes to journey to know and believe— as total truth.

In the span of a night of communal celebration, each of us brought into focus an aspect of what we believed as a personal truth. The DJs would construct a musical journey that would build to a crescendo of celebratory passion, to musical heights, that would connect us, in the most intimate of ways, and then gradually bring us back down to planet Earth. And over those many hours, which could seem to be a lifetime, we acted our parts on that stage, as the personalities we were, and are, and will be.

For some it was all about dancing and the music, sometimes alone, or sometimes in the embrace of others. For some it was more about the hunt. Looking for a sexual encounter or looking for a lover. For some it was about the escape. It was either an escape from the "real life" transpiring outside the walls of *The Roxy*, or from even the reality of the dance floor itself. Drugs and alcohol were the chosen escape vehicles and even here the choices varied. For some, it was guilty pleasure. For others, a lonely commune.

CENTER OF THE UNIVERSE

There were twelve of us—all Beings of Light, who came together upon the stage, this earthly plane, each wrapped in his own confusions, filled with yearning and denial, impersonating the unique role we each chose for this masquerade. It was not by chance or coincidence that our paths crossed and our lives intersected and intertwined. For the plan is far deeper than what appears on the surface. Exploring love, as the design of our journeys required, meant bringing into focus those experiences created by our shared illusions. Our individual curriculums were realized in our shared school. We each entered at different levels of coursework from grade school through post-graduate; we each progressed at our own speed, all the while helping one another along. Why these twelve? We are drawn to those souls we have loved before, those who we have known in prior incarnations. We come together to help remind each other of who we are, as we freely explore love within the blueprint of this life.

Our personalities were formed from our earliest childhood environments of home and family, creating a concept of life that we each could then take, along with our minds and our emotions, on our individual shared adventures. Along the way, we altered our personalities, subjecting them to the perceived demands of others—parents, siblings, teachers, friends, and lovers. And to the extent that fear took us by the hand to keep us safe, we entered further into the illusion, further into darkness, and further from truth. The particulars of our formative years, those determining moments in a life, often filled with struggle, can be viewed as sand on the shores of our histories. Other than helping us enter into the illusion with our own limited view of self, they are of no import. In truth, the journey we each have embarked on is in large part designed to free us from those historical limitations. Lives touching upon lives along the way help to unshackle the chains we have placed upon ourselves. We might be loathe to admit it, when we believe those lives have brought us pain. Taking responsibility for the pain of one's life eliminates blame.

Suffice it to say that each of us suffered the pangs of separation. Initially we separated from Oneness. Our individuated consciousnesses embarked on journeys of exploration and discovery in physicality. We left the greater reality of our true home. We separated from our God and entered the womb. Then, at birth, we separated from the womb. It was only then that we became fearful of others. We saw Oneness as the cause of separation. We aligned ourselves with physicality and our forgetting deepened in the moment, as we completely entered our illusion.

On center stage of my universe, the cast is Wagnerian. But the key souls in my story, friends and lovers, Angels all, are the Beings of Life who have traveled as my companions in this and our many other incarnations, closely aligning their trajectories with mine for various moments in time. Each one of us is a unique soul whose way of denying light and truth, in this life, is particular to that soul's journey. And each of us experiences and explores love in that individual context and manner. Each soul chooses only one or two areas defined by their requisite negativities in which to experience the beliefs it holds to be true. There is some comfort in realizing that all souls, no matter the costume, humble or high, peasant or pope, pauper or king, are all winding their way along lighted paths of apparent and varying confusions to the benefit of their own enlightenment.

My companions and I all have amazing hearts, although with varying layers of encrustation surrounding them, and varying depths of forgetfulness appended to them. But, with that at our core, I have kept heart in our names. I was *Wounded Heart*. Then there were *Distant Heart, Worried Heart, Punished Heart, Fearful Heart, Lonely Heart, Empty Heart, Scared Heart, Betrayed Heart, Scarred Heart, Lost Heart,* and *Dark Heart*. Together our individual and collective consciousness created an illusion—the physically-manifested dream of our collaboration in the center of the Universe, at *The Roxy*. In forming our relationships, we each did visit and dwell, for varying moments, in the illusion of another. There I experienced other truths and distortions, not those of my soul's fundamental belief, which played across our shared stage. Fear can be very compelling as it whispers its warnings across many illusions. In that context, I also spent some time experiencing guilt, pride, and vanity along the way. I would so fully enter another's illusion that I would engage in battle with their demons, even as I experienced my own—a most painful education. But as *Wounded*, I chose in the moment as best and in the only way I could.

So first then, of this band of adventurers, there was myself. Since I am comfortable in more openly sharing my particular journey of self-discovery, I begin with my impersonation, as I bare my own soul. I chose the role of *Wounded*. My good-hearted personality had at its core a need to validate self-worth through acts of giving. There was no doubting my noble purpose except that my giving eventually became, in every instance, self-sacrifice. To give with an open heart is pure joy. Anything less can become a burden. So, as my need to help my other struggling angels became burdensome, I would invariably find myself wounded, hurt by my own "good intentions". And in giving over my selfhood to others I became powerless. Self-love was disguised as love for others. And that was my distortion and my confusion. Abdicating my power for the role of *Wounded*, I could never find my true "noble self". I could only find a semblance of real self-love. Hence, there was always someone who was responsible for my pain. And invariably it was the less-than-grateful recipient who I had chosen to help. And so it was, as I gazed into their confused eyes, asking them to tell me who I was and how loved I was, that they disappointed me, time and time again, with their measure of my worth, as best as they could return it to me. And I allowed myself to feel betrayed by Love and diminished by them. And so, each relationship would end with hurt and disappointment and varying degrees of recriminations and blame. How could such a loving, good-hearted man, such as I, always wind up with others, who I so misjudged, who were so much less than what I deserved and so much less loving than the promise they offered? Well, of course, the false promise was of my own making. The answer, now obvious, is that I was experiencing Love in the manner of the belief I held to be true in the consciousness of my soul. I believed I needed them to make me whole, to make me feel valued, to make me feel loved. But in truth, they could never verify me. They did not know who they are, let alone who I am. I needed to experience the pain of rejection and the hurt of dismissal, in the exact manner I did, in order to find true love of self. And with love for self, I found compassion for self and for my journey as well.

On the dance floor of *The Roxy*, I would often act as master of ceremonies or cruise director. I would gather the "faithful" in my group, bypass the line that wound down the block, going directly to Derek, at the door, who would greet us and wave us past the velvet rope. And it was there that I did indeed meet a lover or two as I played my part. Needless to say, when it was over, I was "***Wounded***".

Along the way, I did align myself with the trajectories of others. And in so doing, I came to both love them and feel true compassion for their struggles. For they are me. And it was through the experiencing of my truths, distortions, and confusions that my resistance was worn away by the painful struggles I created, to arrive at a point where Light and true pleasure were waiting there for me. There I found love of self, love of others, gentleness, and compassion as I began to lay claim to my Self, my Life, my Light, my Truth, and my God.

I no longer chastise my guests. I, as host, bore sole responsibility for the party I was throwing at my own expense. My traveling companions helped release me from the limiting historical garb I cloaked myself in, as I did help them as well. When the education is complete, and the release as fully realized as it can be, all the gifts available in the relationship have been given. Then, it is as it should be, our souls and consciousnesses twirl away, figuratively on the dance floor of *The Roxy* and more literally, as our paths take their own twists and turns on our journeys to selfhood.

Punished was a most loving and dear sweet heart. He, however, had the belief that he deserved punishment. And since the physical incarnation manifested on this earthly plane allows for the belief to be experienced, what he held in his heart was brought into his life. And he developed AIDS, the illness where everything in one's environment is to be feared, because all of it can hurt you. The immune compromise leaves you defenseless, so that even air, and water, and love can harm you. It is the sternest of teachers. Yet it brings the hope of eventual and ultimate realization that one is worthy of one's own love. All his judgments were self-judgments. For sweet *Punished*, there was never anything that required forgiveness. He was perfect imperfection from the moment of his birth. As I entered his illusion, I did indeed do battle with his virus—as his lover and his doctor. And as his health deteriorated, my willingness to give my life over to his care became a burden that I carried. It started more innocently as the anticipated joyful relationship filled with youthful sexual abandon morphed into its antithesis. And with this, the life I imagined changed forever. Anyone who has been faced with the role of caregiver knows the burdensome choices of which I speak. And in the aftermath of his death, I did carry the weight of survivor. So where does one choose to say, "Enough"? When is it all right to stake out one's claim to the life one wishes to have? Is the decision to turn away from another's painful illusion ever a loving choice? I chose to stay, and give the care and comfort I could, believing that my "noble self-sacrifice" was the only choice I could make. Yet I cursed the fates and the God I did not yet believe in for his painful death, our loss of innocence, and my own suffering and pain. We together (or I alone) bore no responsibility for the events of our creation, for awareness was not yet perceived; blame still needed to be affixed!

While initially, he did spend a moment or two on the dance floor at *The Roxy*, his punishment in part involved avoiding further involvement in that communal atmosphere. So he would stay home as the rest of our group continued to amuse themselves.

Fearful, too, had a most loving heart. He was fully immersed in his role. He would walk in light, yet see only his shadow. His life was his master, not his child. And the difficulty in thoroughly embracing a life that cannot be understood, but only lived, presented great difficulties for one who was so fully limited by his five senses. He was filled with rules. They provided an illusion of safety. He lived within structure to comfort his fears. And in the name of fear he could not move beyond his structure. The distortion of his forgetting was the fear he experienced. And in the shadow of that fear, this beautiful human being became precisely what it was that he feared. Fear motivated him but it never solved anything. Any pain, illness, or discomfort he developed came from fear. Yet, pain was not his truth and suffering was not his reality. You only have one lens through which to view life in any one moment. Whether constricted or expanded, it takes a great deal of faith to be human.

More than anyone, he reveled in the musical journey and the very act of dancing.

Scared was afraid to be seen for who he was. So vanity became him. That mirror that he held out before him was the only loving connection he could offer. Beneath it always lurked the fear that there was nothing else of value.

He would dance in the most guarded of ways, only allowing in those whose outward beauty stroked his vanity and made him feel special.

Distant had as his distortion the armor he wore. By removing himself from entering fully into the full rough and tumble of relationships and life, he protected himself from anticipated rejections and humiliations. His journey of learning to celebrate life with pleasure as truth was a distant memory from a locked–away treasure chest.

He would dance with almost everyone for the briefest of moments, then move on to the next beneficiary of his presence.

Lonely always seemed disconnected from his companions, even in the intimacy of shared moments. He, too, had a loving and giving heart. But there were strings attached. To offer too much love was a dangerous thing. If he did, he would leave himself defenseless. By making demands in exchange, he answered fear's call. Then, he would not be so exposed. Then, he would have some leverage to employ when hurt inevitably came to visit his heart.

While he did dance with his friends, more often he was either dancing alone, or, if he found someone new, he couldn't be found. He would be off in another corner of the dance floor, where he could not be seen.

Empty, as with all the Beings of Light, was filled with love. He had so much to give but not enough left for self. Simply, he had an emptiness that dearly required another angel to make him whole. But outwardly searching for what was to be found in his heart would be the exploration of his distortion, and not the solution to his quest.

He would tend to stand at the bar, watching over the scene and waiting for someone to come over and join him.

Betrayed was a most sensitive soul who could not accept life on its own terms. To that extent he was betrayed by life, or so he thought. In order to touch beauty he found solace in the escape of drugs which, while providing an initial moment of respite, became a cruel and unforgiving addiction from which there seemed to be no escape. The false pleasure would be recognized for what it was when he would fail himself; make himself sick; do foolish, destructive things. It was then that he knew he had betrayed himself. His journey back into the flow of life was to go where there was real pleasure with love of self, love of others; seeing others with gentleness and compassion.

Not surprisingly, he spent a good deal of time going back and forth from the bar to the dance floor to the bathroom and back again.

Scarred was so hurt by his painful entry into illusion that he was afraid to love fully. A childhood of abuse, both emotional and physical, was the parental detritus of distorted love that he was taught. Much like a honey bee going from flower to flower seeking nectar, he would seek to know the nectar of love in its many guises. He would speak of love as avoidance and as a defense for his own "unlovingness" while at the same moment touching it as best he could. In moments of knowing he would bridge the divide between divinity and humanity, and in an instant forget and choose fear instead of Love.

He was probably the most gregarious of all, both within and outside our group. He met people with ease and charmed them all. He was fearless.

Lost was lost through fragmentation. While we all individuate our consciousness into physicality, *Lost* further fragmented sex from love, to the degree that sex could only be experienced through very convoluted and distorted and dark channels. The exploration of Love through this particular distortion makes a most difficult situation for anyone looking to enjoy a sense of Oneness in a relationship with one such as *Lost*.

Strangely enough *Lost* could often not be found, as he was often having sexual encounters where they might be had.

Dark brought great confusion and turmoil. He chose darkness in his denial of Light and in stepping out to bear witness to his distortions, he brought rage, violence, and cruelty. But beneath his anger was fear. And beneath his fear was yearning. The pain of his creation led directly to his illusion of darkness within. Although he denied responsibility for his pain, without the pain there would be no issue of responsibility. It was from those depths that he would have to begin to disentangle his dank distortions back into the flow of Light and truth. Although it was difficult to see his loving heart, we did share love for a moment. Once the love is there, it is present forevermore in eternity.

He might be found dancing only in his underwear, having misplaced his clothing in his attempt to connect with people as best as he could.

Now, knowing their names makes my eventual disappointment as **Wounded** more easily understood. If you were to gaze into the eyes of anyone whose individual context and manner is thusly described, what kind of validation can be offered? **Punished, Worried, Fearful, Lonely, Empty, Scared, Betrayed, Distant, Scarred, Lost, Dark**. Clearly, only a muddled "validation", coming from the perspective of those particular confusions, can be offered back.

Yet all these relationships of my life, "failed" or otherwise, did teach and instruct me. It was through those experiences that my life was created. Eventually the cumulative events in that life led me to yearn for something more—as I began to turn to Light.

The dance floor at *The Roxy* allowed each to dance with me, and one another, as we spun together and apart, as our trajectories aligned and diverged. And from the heights of knowing, my greater wisdom could see this all as the inevitable journey honoring my soul's intent. All the while, I would enjoy the blinding moments of love's glory only to suffer the deepest depths of despair, as love was explored with wild abandon and painful loss, in those eleven-plus variations.

Now, with the benefit of hindsight, I would not choose to enter another's illusion to battle illusory demons. If I were to enter another's illusion now, it would be to fully share in the love, joy and happiness that we each brought to the feast of life. The exploration and self-discovery in that context would not spring from the lack of self-love but from its very truth. To those whose journeys still wind their way in darkness, I offer my Light and my truth, and my full measure of loving compassion.

Those Beings of Light helped free me from my historical chains, which limited me to believing I was the costume that I wore to impersonate who I really am.

At this moment, I am finally free. Free from limitation, free to be who I really am, and free from fear's grip to which I clung so tightly. I am free to let my experiences create my life, trusting in the knowledge and eternal wisdom of the perfect Love that surrounds us all. I have, in large part, finally surrendered to my own reality and my own integrity. That is free choice in the truest sense, as surrender stands in bold relief against the backdrop of historical conformity.

Of course, until one is able to live in the moment of NOW, in order to escape one's creation, one's mind wanders through the colorless environment of distant memory or tries to inhabit an imagined happy future of what is yet to be created.

With the closing of *The Roxy*, the center of my universe moved—to where I am now fully certain it remains—into my heart.

Near the end I began to doubt my own sanity as reality as I knew it morphed into something greater than I ever imagined. Who might imagine that freedom, truth, beauty, and love might all be found so close—within my own heart?

There is not one of us who at some point does not question who we really are. What is our role in life? What are we supposed to do? Who are we supposed to become? With such questioning come fears, and doubts, and worries along with disillusionments and disappointments. There is not one of us who does not suffer the loss of a childhood hope or ambition. With such a backdrop, it should not be at all surprising that we then suffer illness, from either emotional or physical disease, as a manifestation of the painful dysfunction we endure. But there is balm for the pain and real pleasure in the very next moment…

It was in my home that my first contact with greater reality occurred. As I cradled **Punished**, his body in my arms, the soul of my long-term lover departed with the rattle of death in his wake. Between sobs and tears, I pleaded that if at all possible he give me a sign, any sign, that he was still with me in death—that there was more to life beyond death. To this he nodded his accord as he ended his life and left this earthly plane.

While standing in his shower the following morning, I did experience the "mini-miracle of the spinning showerhead," memorialized previously in *a Book of Life*. As the water stopped hitting my back, I turned to witness the showerhead spinning clockwise with the inner plastic piece spinning counter-clockwise. In that moment, filled with sorrow and love, joy filled my being as I recognized this as the sign I had asked for. I have never been able to reproduce that magical moment, despite years of twisting and turning faucets and showerheads. Yet, it was in that shower that I began what I have come to refer to as "Shower Conversations with God."

For it was there that I began asking out loud the overarching questions of life's meaning and purpose; from there answers began to be heard. It is not too surprising that at one moment or another, all of my "Hearts", following a night of dancing at *The Roxy*, have had occasion to use that very shower. Their questions are my questions, for in truth, we are all ONE. A bridge between spirit truth and human "reality", I offer the answers I heard—understandings of what I now know, as I have "Reawakened". So, enjoy the showering experience; the water temperature is divine.

If one is about to converse with God, it seems sensible to have some concept of whom or with what one is conversing. Is it a conversation with self? Is it like prayer? Or is it more like meditation? So, how is one to think of God? One can try to make any human image one wishes, as religion often does. And while I am not speaking against religion, for it too, can offer a way to explore love, I would suggest something more believable. I prefer to think of God as a higher truth, a wider reality, innate and natural order, Divine safety and love, eternal reality, a Universal Soul of All-That-Is, the All-Seeing Consciousness of Love with a power beyond anything that anyone has ever touched. It is that core of God that is the essence of who we are. And it is that which speaks to us. And it is that voice with which I converse. When I feel true joy and fulfillment it is my heart that knows God's will—for it is my own. To find the way to joy and fulfillment is to hear my heart despite the din and through the cacophony of other voices within me. Those are the voices of fear, rage, jealousy, contradiction, and obstinacy, along with all the other illusions and confusions we all have brought to the journey. When those other voices have been stilled, we can begin to surrender to our own reality and our own integrity. The ultimate surrender will be to God's will as manifested in our own hearts. Until love of self begins to take hold there can be no surrender to our own reality. So, the concept of surrender to God's will as manifested in our hearts will remain only words on a page. Until the process of turning to Light has begun, it is not possible. Until you believe that what you hope is true is indeed the truth, it is not possible. The requisite level of awareness necessary to transform those words into true feelings, with a measure of understanding, comes only with the cumulative erosions of fear's defenses that encrust one's loving heart. That erosion occurs through the experiences we bring to our lives. So, the best those words can offer, before one's heart is free, is a willingness to believe, without the necessity of doing so yet.

There is magic all around us. There is a divine spark within each of us. But what the mind does not see, the heart may not believe. Yet, it is what it already knows.

Most all of us are familiar with the short tale by Hans Christian Andersen, "The Emperor's New Clothes." In the tale, an emperor, who cares only for his attire, hires two weavers who promise him the finest suit of clothes from a fabric that is invisible to anyone who is either "just hopelessly stupid," or unfit to occupy his own position in life. Unable to see the cloth himself, and fearing that he might appear unfit to be emperor or just stupid, he pretends he can see the fabric. Dressed in mime by the charlatans, he then marches before his subjects in a grand procession. It is not until a child in the crowd announces that the Emperor is wearing nothing at all that the others in the crowd take up the child's cry. The Emperor, wincing in embarrassment, suspects he has heard the truth, but continues to march proudly along in the procession.

Seeing what is before you, believing it to be truth, denying the truth of what you see, or convincing yourself that what you see is something different is all part of the journey. At what moment does something that you have known and seen time and time again become the reality of your truth? At the moment in time when your soul in its greater wisdom decides it is time to turn.

In this manner, all souls that incarnate are on their own individual paths to self-discovery. And knowing this should tell each of us to believe our own hearts. Whether a renowned physicist announces that the universe could self-create without God, or a pope or imam tells the only way to get to heaven is to follow them, know that each is winding his own personal way through his own particular confusion, to come to the same moment of truth, as are we all.

Once the turn has begun, nothing ever seems quite the same. One can see magic all around. People begin to appear more like souls occupying a personality. Compassion for self and for others grows. Love changes everything. A connection to the Earth is felt anew. And again, there is an eternity of more.

And, why do we exist? We exist by the very miracle of Love. We ARE. There is no other why. To personalize that a bit more, YOU ARE. And since we are all one, I AM. There is a point of intersection of science and spirituality. And that point is belief. What do you choose to believe? Where does belief so resonate with your being that you accept it as truth? Before the physically-manifested universe came into being, there was a void. So, even with science as your god, there is a point at which you believe that from nothingness came this universe. In that very belief, there is magic. One can place belief at many different points along a continuum of creation such as a big bang cosmological theory starting with a singularity when the fabric of space and time began. That would seem to be a magical occurrence. Is I AM any less magical or any less believable? Well, that is what we have come to explore, is it not?

There are all levels of teaching and understanding available here on earth. Hear what resonates with your intuitive perceptions. Find your affinity there. Read this story and understand it on as many levels as you are able. In each perception there is truth. Follow each truth in its own level of perception as each thread forms the totality of the fabric of God's consciousness which is Perfect Love.

Human physically-manifested reality exists on a compatible level of consciousness. And consciousness creates its own reality. Hence, we all look like human beings, so alike yet so very different in so many ways, whatever our level of awareness may be in any moment, whatever the reality we bring to our existence. Human physicality offers a foundation for spiritual needs to take hold. All that exists in human experience mirrors the spirit's situation. It is the mirror image of the inner self that is found in the outer reality of our creation that is our life. The mirror offered on this earthly plane is to reflect back as experiences those beliefs that form our curriculum for a lifetime. What is it that the soul wants to know? What is it that consciousness must see? And, as it denies its longing, it yearns for more. As we create our truths and our distortions we learn. So, we absorb self into Self, and finally into God.

So, why ever leave God to come to this messy planet? It is to return with greater light and understanding. Without the experience of individuation and separation there would always be totality without the consciousness to experience and express. With that barren bit made fully fertile in the process, we become a part of the whirling universe, unfolding in the moment, at the leading edge of eternal creation.

The gathering of all experience is to know the nature of the love within. That is why from the point of view of All-That-Is, there is no bad or wrong experience. Right or wrong do not exist as absolutes. They are perceptions from different points of understanding. In the moment, you can make no wrong choice. Hindsight, of course, is to recognize that in the next moment of NOW, you would choose differently.

The power of fear is strong and seductive; the belief in darkness is compelling; the idea that rage can trump the power of love screams out across the globe. It is these beliefs that we brought with us into this world which we have come to alter. Nothing exists beyond the need for love to remember itself and there is an eternity of more. As love learns to love itself, it creates itself in its own image. The issues of life are of no importance yet the experiences one brings to one's life are of paramount importance to the individual. And, eventually, whispers of truth become paramount in their importance in the human life. This planet was formed with love to honor the forgetting of who we are; to experience love where love seems not to be. We did not come to think or understand our way through life, we came to live it. The very hope of understanding the core of eternal wisdom dusts it again with limitation. So, wisdom is putting mind in service of the heart. Enlightenment is bridging spirit reality and human illusion, with the knowledge that we exist in eternity as a conscious being, that spirit exists, that God exists. Living is fully and completely experiencing our own divinity. The separation from and return to God is the creative pulse of the universe. There is consciousness in all things and the flow of consciousness is towards Light. The only resistance is in one's own consciousness. There will be a moment in eternity that all humankind eventually and individually does reach. After living through a sufficient number of reincarnational cycles, the soul turns towards Light. This moment comes when the soul is ready to reverse course and begin the journey home. This compelling image is something you would think all would hope for in their lives. But some souls don't even yet know that they are in school, let alone just starting kindergarten. For those with greater awareness, the moment still cannot be sped up by altering behavior.

It is not behavior-based, nor is it within the ability of the mind. It is a matter of the heart and the willingness to believe and choose Love instead of fear. The moment each reaches this point is individual in its manner. And it is the cumulative, individual life experiences of each soul that eventually wears away resistance that smooths the yearning and allows the turning.

If you are reading this now, you have started the turn to seek Light.

When we yearn for something more, there is a willingness to believe that there must be something more. There is also the deeply-held hope that what we would wish to be true is indeed true. Trust is not required to turn to seek Light. It will happen as it will of its own accord. But with the turning, there is a moment when fundamental trust does take hold. Trust in truth; freedom from fear; belief in God Supreme.

And when the very last soul has fully and completely experienced its own divinity, then our earth will return Home in a glorious blaze of light.

So we move from Oneness, with Oneness, as we are Oneness.

Incarnating into human physicality with its illusion of beginning and end provides a false template of reality to the intellect. This "reality" of all things having a beginning and end poses an impossible task for the intellect, which demands explanation and understanding to believe the primary reality of all things without the illusion of ending. For the heart it is recognition of truth, known at a deeper level by the human consciousness, as a memory that must be reclaimed. The understanding of eternity is within grasp of the heart but not the intellect. One can touch it when saying Yes to the moment of NOW.

There is little doubt in my mind that the spiritual teachings delivered to humanity over the time of our known history are complete. With this availability of teaching and understanding, every soul may ascend the ladder of awareness and ultimately graduate from this earthly classroom. How these teachings are understood and incorporated into one's life will depend on many things. First comes the yearning for something more than the reality of one's life. Then, there is the willingness of any individual to believe that there is something worth knowing in terms of spiritual truth. But "understanding" is commensurate with the level of awareness that one brings to the table. While the information is "out there", I do believe that tailoring the delivery to the zeitgeist of the moment plays an important role in making for a more resonant presentation.

The desire to turn to the Light manifests in the first moment of questioning, "Is this all there is?" The hope that "There must be something more," echoes long-forgotten memories of a deeply held truth of a Greater Reality.

Now even if one denies all that I am about to present, the end result still would be a more harmonious world wherein individuals are all maximizing their angelic natures, with clear benefit to mankind and the earth we occupy. Whether this is simply a utopian dream or fantasy, or the inevitable pulsation of the universe is where belief enters.

Understanding the true meaning of things doesn't alter one's journey or the emotional impact of events as they are experienced. The journey is far too compelling and life far too well designed. It does, however, accelerate the learning process. Knowing the fabric of God's consciousness, which is LOVE, and the state of grace you occupy truly leads to awe and humility, a realization of how small yet how significant one is. It is with a great sense of self and Self and with great humility that one shares the spark. The self that you eventually come to love still stumbles and still grows. You know that you are only at the beginning of an eternal process of growth as you yearn to become what you already are—a God-realized Being, participating at the cutting edge of creation.

Acceptance of this cannot be taught. It cannot be forced. It cannot be practiced. It will occur and can only occur through accumulated life experiences in as many accumulated incarnations as a soul requires, the reincarnational wheel wearing away the negativity and denial of the reality of God.

We all have an aura or energy that surrounds us—the glow of greater Self. Certain energies engender more widespread recognition, as with very charismatic individuals. We all seek and respond to the auras that are more in tune with our own. Imagine each aura as a single note. The musical metaphor can start with an eighty-eight-key piano. Each note represents an individual in a small community of eighty-eight souls. Any individual's note can be pitch perfect or it may be sharp or flat or totally out of key. For perfect harmony, you would want all eighty-eight notes tuned to perfection. Unfortunately, there is no one piano tuner to accomplish this. Each note must tune itself. Each individual in this imaginary community can only strive to be that crystal-clear, perfectly-pitched note that is unique to them. Initially, the importance of playing in harmony, let alone tuning one's note, may be irrelevant. For the purpose of a piano may not be obvious to the untrained ear. But the inestimable joy of music eventually takes hold.

In the process of the soul's journey through human life it is the wearing away of resistance and the turning to Light that takes hold. The eighty-eight souls each individually tune their unique note as they reach a new level of awareness, perhaps not aware that in the oneness of the piano there will be a blending of all into one.

Some notes on our metaphorical piano will harmonize perfectly. Others, not so much. And so with human beings, our auras or energies or unique notes, many harmonize beautifully, or not so much. And when a soul departs human form in death, their note may still echo and reverberate for a time beyond their passing.

Now, take those notes, and associate each with a color—a musical color. This lighted piano now becomes a rainbow of Light. Now extend that imaginary community to the billions of people on Earth, each with their own note of light. The process of tuning occurs even without the awareness that it is taking place at all. However, once that awareness takes hold, along with striving to be the best note you can, the process accelerates. As others see the Light of your uniqueness, it adds impetus to their own journey to be that crystal-clear note that is their own. With a unique color for each being on Earth, it becomes spectacularly difficult to envision this vision of beauty.

All things are Light. Love is Light. Truth is Light. When one remembers, the hidden Light begins to glow. Like a flashlight, you can shine your Light where you go. You can illuminate caves of darkness, where others are so far removed from truth and Light that they cannot see. Once you have that flashlight, you can't lose it and it doesn't go out. You can trip or stumble or stray from the path, but the Light remains with you and you still illuminate where you go. That spark is available to everyone, although it may be difficult to believe. There are those for whom the absence of Light is so profound that they cannot see the value of human life, where the divinity of our souls does not exist. Those, whose God-denying acts of cruelty, torture, murder, or martyrdom are so far removed from the sweet kiss that life can be, believe that heaven can be reached bypassing human existence. In truth, heaven can be found within you at any moment.

We all tend to look to others for approval as we tailor our responses to gain that approval. We look to others to tell us who we are and all the while they are looking to us for the same reason. And in the mix, everyone is a bit lost and adrift.

Many of life's seminal moments can be viewed as an on/off light switch. There is much layering to this analogy. The first is from darkness to light in a figurative sense. There are also literal moments of great change when it seems as though a switch has been flipped. These changes can take place in others as it affects us or in ourselves. But it is probably fair to say that anytime a switch seems to have been flipped, there is growth taking place. For accompanying the literal is also that figurative change to a state of awareness that allows for more light, even if one sits with one's eyes closed!

One of life's most difficult tasks is switching back the internal switch from other-directed to self-directed. This is not a selfish or egotistical statement. It is one of the greatest of personal accomplishments—the fulfillment of a promise. To look within oneself for "perfect love" that is usually sought in others is indeed life's journey. It is no wonder that oftentimes one may wind up disappointed, if not heartbroken, when a relationship fails and that perfect love turns out to be less than perfect. The nearly insurmountable difficulty is that happiness and joy don't necessarily show up at the moment the switch is flipped. Initially it is a leap of faith. To fully embrace not only the concept but the reality of finding God within is the final leg of the transformative journey. That is the Reawakening—the moment when one starts to recall one's own divinity. What could be simpler or more magical? To realize that life's entire journey is at long last to simply flip a switch! Clearly, God does have a sense of humor. So, the light switch is the life switch.

With ascension up the ladder of awareness, and with wisdom and enlightenment, everything changes, yet all is the same. You may see beyond knowing, yet life must still be experienced. The blueprint of the soul's journey must still be honored. You cannot understand All-That-Is, for it has a vastness that is incomprehensible and a consciousness beyond understanding. All you can do is follow your heart, which knows your soul better than your mind could possibly dream; to strive in perfect yearning, knowing that you are surrounded by Perfect Love.

Know that there is Divine Law of Truth, Balance, Unity, Order, and Cause and Effect.

There, you have it… And it is lost again…

If I were to choose three words of "wisdom", they would be leap, yes, and now.

They are different for every individual. "Leap" means to follow one's own heart, having put the mind in service of the heart. It means being fearless, secure in the belief that there is nothing to worry about. Of course, hearing the voice of one's heart requires a bit of experience. And everyone's experience is different. If one is leaping for any other reason, it's not wisdom, but another experience to learn from.

"Yes" means saying yes to the moment, no matter what is transpiring either personally or in the world at large. It is recognition that what you are experiencing, you are manifesting, so your consciousness may see what you believe. In accepting this, you realize its importance to yourself. If you are experiencing pain and suffering, well then that is what you believe is necessary in the moment. Eventually, you will move through the experience, as you transform what you believe. And if you don't believe this, you will soon enough.

"Now" is where you exist. When you are centered in who you are, and exist in the moment of Now, you are in truth. And in truth, you touch eternity.

When your heart, mind, body, and soul are aligned in the moment of Now, you truly are free. Free not only from all the human distortions of fear, and illness, and aging, and death—for none of them can harm you. In the eternal consciousness that you are, you are free from the reincarnational cycles on this earthly plane. You are free to explore other realms as your creativity unfolds. You are free to reconnect your image with the Oneness of all things. You are free to go home as you have reawakened to your own divinity, binding self to greater Self to God in the Oneness of All-That-Is.

Perhaps you may now know our paths did not cross by accident. I hope my story has been able to touch you—to bring a joyful tear to your countenance, happiness to your heart, and a resonance to your soul consciousness. When I write what is heartfelt, I am in the moment of NOW. If you say YES, and share that with me, then I am transformed back into who I already AM, as are you.

It is all about LOVE...

AN ANGEL'S SONG

Love everybody, love everything.
Love everybody, love everyone.
This is God. This is Love.
This is God. This is Love.
God is Love. God is Love.

ACKNOWLEDGMENTS

My thanks to David Ballard, Guy Smith, and Javier Morgado for help in copy-editing this book; to Niceto Festin and Ken Schaefer for their insightful advice. Special thanks go to Jonathan Jurcev for his invaluable suggestions and help in editing this book.

Artwork sketch was a gift from the author's parents on the occasion of his graduation from The Mount Sinai School of Medicine; artwork drawn by Claire Scheiner.

Sunset photograph of the Great South Bay in Fire Island, New York taken by George Trapp.

Special thanks to Russell Brown and Javier Justiniano for letting me see things from different perspectives of understanding—allowing me to share thoughts and feelings as we remind one another of who we really are.

I have been blessed with many loving extended family members, amazing friends, and many wonderful and not so wonderful lovers. There are too many in the first two categories to mention all, and I would, without doubt, inadvertently neglect someone in such an exhaustive naming. Having said that, I nevertheless single out a few. I recognize Mark, with whom I still, after forty years, share a loving bond of friendship. He, his wife Donna, and their son Aaron, have been linchpins in my life.

Jason and Sheldon were prized friends of my childhood. They were also early and valuable signposts, offering hints of roads yet to be travelled.

Javier was an "old soul" at nineteen, when we first met. He is a terrific friend. He has been there through the good times and the bad. He has offered his support and love without reserve. He is family.

And in this context of friendships, there is Willy, whose astute perspective, talent, and caring have never failed me.

There are two friends whose trajectories have intersected, travelled parallel to, and diverged from mine along the way. One is another Mark. The threads of friendship may have been frayed, but the fabric of love has endured. He too retains a special place in my heart and in my life.

And there is another Jason. Without his love, I would have plumbed the depths of despair far longer than needed. And thankfully, he remains a vital part of my life as well.

There was also a unique and special group, who came together, and collaborated with me, so that my play "And The Stars Were Shining…" could be given life on the stage. This group was bound together then, and to varying degrees have maintained a closeness that is still magical, not just with me, but with one another. My gratitude and love goes to all those who made that moment possible, especially Bobby, Caleb, Diana, Guy, Malan, Mariano, Niceto, Stephen, and Steven. From that essential core were forged close bonds of uniquely special friendships. They know who they are and of what I speak.

The wonderful lovers of my life are a select group. Where shared moments of passionate love flourished, whether fleeting, enduring, joy-filled or painful, our trajectories aligned. I lovingly acknowledge Brent, Tom, Ron, Niceto, and Michael. Each embodies facets of me—the facets that existed and needed to be experienced in those moments. If I were to fragment into multiple personalities, those bits of self can be found in each one of them. So, I experienced the different facets of self through others who I brought into my life. There were moments when I loved them (and myself) and brought joy into those moments. There were other moments when self-loathing, pain, and hurt were the creations. And in those fleeting moments, it was a denial of love (hate) that came to visit.

Each, in his own exceptional way, added so much richness to this life. Brent's love and life was the crucible. Therein was forged the theme of meaning and purpose—fused to existence and questioning God. Tom gave me an early glimpse of loving Oneness— reawakening my passion with the rediscovery of love and its power. With Ron, I was forced to rediscover love of self and compassion for the difficult journeys of others. Niceto's angelic soul had returned forgiveness and constant love, even with the pain I caused. What an amazing gift and what a beautiful lesson from a Being of Light. Michael, with whom I shared so much passion and so many hopes and dreams, was the catalyst for more fully realizing who I am. It was from him that I came to realize that when there is love, all love is true. Where lovers brought unduly painful experiences to my life, I do now embrace those experiences as well as their roles. It was all a necessary part of my growth and my life. All have helped bring me to this perfect moment. I am so very thankful to them all for sharing their lives with me.

ABOUT THE AUTHOR

Howard Lawrence Scheiner was born to modest beginnings and raised with love in New York City. A graduate of The Mount Sinai School of Medicine, he feels privileged to practice medicine. He shares a busy practice in Manhattan with his medical partner of thirty-plus years, specializing in Internal Medicine and HIV Medicine. Combining many loves, he founded "The Brent Varner Project, Inc.," a charity that provides free HIV services to those in need through The Actors Fund of America.

Through a close association as a major donor to Broadway Cares/ Equity Fights AIDS, he had the opportunity to appear on stage in many Broadway and Off-Broadway shows. His love of people and theater culminated in his own Off-Broadway play, "And the stars were shining…," which he wrote, directed, and produced at the Jose Quintero theater in 2002.

A life-long love of music and a bit of inexplicable inspiration can be found in his recently composed "Genesis Sonata" for piano. It had its public debut in 2009, and he happily shares it on youtube.com. The tantalizing possibility that it might be choreographed into a ballet thrills him.

Of note, he awakes each day happy to be alive, feeling blessed with all the joys and sorrows of his life, joyfully connected to All-That-Is and thoroughly savoring his singular journey. With greater understanding came a new perspective. "A Book of Life-Welcome to a Greater Reality," was and is the story of his personal journey to understanding and belief in a Greater Reality.

The words he now writes come from this new and different perspective—words that come to him outside his five senses. They come from spirit; from greater wisdom and expanded consciousness. They come with the yielding to and the certainty in fundamental trust. Trust that he is held in the hands of Perfect Love, of All-That-Is. Having glimpsed a light through a door that is barely just unlocked, it will take at least the rest of this life to reach that door and throw it wide open

He remains bound to the city of his birth, residing in Manhattan with Coco the Toy Poodle, Nero the Maltese, and Bobby and Jay the New Roommates, as a new chapter unfolds.